G000300081

LIVERPOOL

A RANDOM HISTORY

An exclusive edition for

This edition first published in Great Britain in 2023 by Allsorted Ltd, Watford, Herts, UK WD19 4BG

The facts and statistics in this book are correct up to the end of the 2022/23 season. The data comes from publicly available sources and is presented as correct as far as our knowledge allows. The opinions in this book are personal and individual and are not affiliated to the football club in any way. Any views or opinions represented in this book are personal and belong solely to the book author and do not represent those of people, institutions or organisations that the football club or publisher may or may not be associated with in professional or personal capacity, unless explicitly stated. Any views or opinions are not intended to malign any religious, ethnic group, club, organisation, company or individual.

All rights reserved. No part of this work may be reproduced in any form or by any means, electronic or mechanical, including photocopying, recording or by any information storage and retrieval system, without the prior written permission of the publisher.

© Susanna Geoghegan Gift Publishing
Author: Magnus Allan
Cover design: Milestone Creative
Contents design: Bag of Badgers Ltd
Illustrations: Ludovic Sallé

ISBN: 978-1-915902-08-5

Printed in China

★ CONTENTS ★

"WHETHER I'M CAPTAIN OR NOT, I ALWAYS LIKE TO THINK THAT I LEAD BY EXAMPLE ANYWAY. I DO THE SAME THINGS AS I ALWAYS DO AND TRY TO HELP THE GROUP OUT."

Jordan Henderson suggests that being a captain is something you are, as well as something you become.

★ INTRODUCTION: ★

GLORY IN RED

Liverpool FC are one of the most famous teams in the history of sport, and their success is central to the identity of the city where they ply their trade. Generations of families have bonded on the terraces of Anfield, giving voice to songs that have inspired amazing performances on the pitch.

There are other teams playing in the city, but it's Liverpool FC, almost as much as the music of the Beatles, that has put the city of Liverpool on the global map.

The history of the club stretches back to the end of the 19th century, but it was the 1960s when the club moved from being one of many football teams to one of sport's global elite – a role the team has strived to retain ever since. Some years, and some teams, are better than others, and there have been tragedies as well as triumphs along the way, but Liverpool FC has always been at the heart of its community, always provided entertainment and always risen to the big occasions.

The story of Liverpool is built on stable finances and a sensible amount of risk, a commitment to the club, long-term strategies for the future and the knowledge that, sometimes, you've just got to go for it. It is also built on the simple joy of football played well, of recognising that sport is a form of entertainment that's nothing if it isn't fun.

Liverpool's role at the heart of its city's community is clear, but it is also a key part of the wider footballing community: Liverpool are consistently the team that the best teams compare themselves to. In most years, the games against Liverpool are the ones that are most likely to define a season.

The Liverpool story is full of true legends. Where else would you find a 30-year chain of managers who delivered an extraordinary level of success that grew out of a modest boot room? Where else but Anfield would you find three words on a simple sign that strike fear into opposition teams, a direct link to one of the Industrial Revolution's most important engineers and one of the most bulging trophy cabinets in all of football?

In some ways, the trouble with Liverpool FC is that there are too many legends, too many stories — but this is a club with history in its heart and the future in its hands. It's a club with fans from all walks of life and from all parts of the globe. Once you've heard the Kop in full voice, once it's found its way into your heart, you'll never walk alone.

·LIVERPOOL·

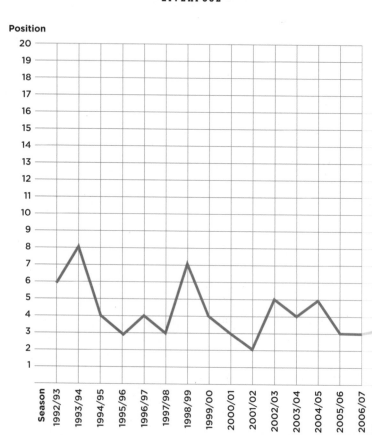

PREMIER LEAGUE
★ FINAL POSITIONS ★

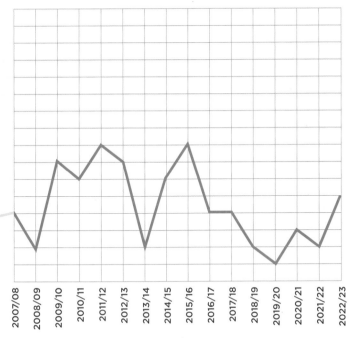

2007/08　2008/09　2009/10　2010/11　2011/12　2012/13　2013/14　2014/15　2015/16　2016/17　2017/18　2018/19　2019/20　2020/21　2021/22　2022/23

★ BILL SHANKLY ★

Bill Shankly changed Liverpool forever. Despite the disruption of World War II, he enjoyed a solid playing career with Carlisle United and Preston North End, but, by all accounts, he always had his sights set on management.

He started his management career with cash-strapped Carlisle, where he spent three seasons guiding them from 15th in the Second Division when he started, to ninth at the second go, before getting to within a whisker of promotion with third place in the 1950/51 season. Disagreements with the board led to his resignation, and he joined third tier Grimsby Town and then Workington before becoming Huddersfield Town's reserve coach. Town were down on their luck after a glorious period in the 1920s and 1930s, and had slipped down into the Second Division in the mid-1950s. He eventually took over, bringing some joy to West Riding, including, on one occasion, delivering a 5–0 drubbing of Liverpool.

When he finally took the reins at Liverpool, the team had similarly been in the Second Division for five years and was struggling on several fronts. However, he spotted potential and quickly formed a rapport with the backroom team of Reuben Bennett, Joe Fagan and Bob Paisley. He embarked on a root-and-branch reform of the entire club, modernising the training facilities, making the most of the youth set-up and completely refreshing the team.

In 1961/62, he brought Liverpool back where they belonged (as champions), and then two years later took them to the pinnacle of the First Division, starting a decade-long run of success that included First Division titles in 1963/64, 1965/66 and 1972/73, FA Cups in 1964/65 and 1973/74, three consecutive FA Charity Shields in 1964, 1965 and 1966 and the UEFA Cup in 1972/73.

The Shankly Gates were erected in his honour.

BILL SHANKLY MOVED THE TEAM TO AN ALL-RED IN 1964; THEY'D PREVIOUSLY PLAYED IN RED SHIRTS AND WHITE SHORTS.

"FOR A PLAYER TO BE GOOD ENOUGH TO PLAY FOR LIVERPOOL, HE MUST BE PREPARED TO RUN THROUGH A BRICK WALL FOR ME THEN COME OUT FIGHTING ON THE OTHER SIDE."

Bill Shankly didn't ask for 110%, he demanded it.

WE NEED TO TALK ★ ABOUT EVERTON ★

History is full of quirks, but here's one for the Liverpool fans out there: Liverpool are one of only three major football clubs to have played in the same stadium since the club was formed. The others are Chelsea and Sheffield United (Newcastle United fans might technically argue that their team deserves a place on this list, but both of their precursor clubs played elsewhere. It's complicated...).

That honour belongs to Everton, who lived at Anfield when they became the third official Football League champions in 1890/91. Preston North End, who had won the first two seasons, came second by two points.

So how did the change come about? Usual rules: personalities, economics and philosophy. Or, to be more specific, a clash of personalities about money with an undertow of philosophical outlooks.

It goes something like this ... Everton had been playing in a field near Stanley Road in the early 1880s until the locals started objecting to the noise and fuss on match days. So John Houlding, a brewer, local councillor and football fan offered to house the Toffees at the new facilities he'd bought from local landowner John Orrell at Anfield, just near Stanley Park, in 1884.

Things were going swimmingly and Everton were very happy in their new home, but over the next six years or so tensions started to rise. There was a feeling that Houlding was doing rather well out of the arrangement: only his beers were being sold at the ground and he was said to have raised the rent from £100 in 1884 to around £250 in 1890. Some of the members of the Everton board were members of the temperance movement that was against the evils of alcohol, so the whole beer thing sat a little uncomfortably with them anyway.

Houlding offered to help Everton turn themselves into a public liability company (plc) and offered to let them buy the ground at Anfield, but the board and several members of the team thought he was charging too high a price and, in October 1891, they made their way to the exit to carry on the story of Everton elsewhere ...

★ BILLY LIDDELL ★

As Liverpool endured its difficult period in the 1950s, the one thing that was almost guaranteed to provide entertainment was Billy Liddell. It was Matt Busby, Liverpool half back and future Manchester United manager, who spotted Liddell playing for Lochgelly Violet FC while off on a golfing trip and talked the Liverpool management into signing him.

He was a stalwart of the Liverpool team that won the First Division in 1946/47, beating second placed Manchester United by a single (but very important) point. The team unfortunately failed to maintain that level of excellence and after a handful of seasons in mid-table, they slipped down to the Second Division at the end of the 1953/54 season. Liddell continued his commitment to the club, delivering more than 30 goals each season in their first two years in the Second Division, and more than 20 each season for the next two seasons. As a result, the club became jokingly known as Liddellpool and the Kop would often erupt with the cry, "Give it to Billy". He received 29 caps for Scotland, finding the net eight times between 1946 and 1955.

On retirement from football, he became a bursar at the University of Liverpool, but continued his relationship with the club. As a season ticket holder.

★ AN EMPTY ANFIELD ★

In 1892, Houlding found himself with a very nice stadium by the standards of the day, but he didn't have a football team to play in it. He was an enterprising Victorian fellow, so he found a way around the problem; he set about forming a new football club.

Now, obviously there is a lot more nuance in the history books, and nothing was as neat as this (particularly given that Houlding appears to have tried to engineer what amounts to a reverse takeover of Everton by registering the name 'Everton Athletic' as a plc with the football authorities before the board had voted their approval for any such move), but right here, 130 odd years later, we face a choice: we can either delve deep into the whole thing and carry on talking about Everton and various Victorian shenanigans, or we can get on with the story of Liverpool.

Houlding, clearly an ambitious man, decided that the bright thing to do would be to name his new club after the entire city rather than a mere suburb, and so, without too much further ado, Liverpool FC was born.

Houlding wasn't on his own, and he had fairly deep pockets, so he loaned Liverpool £500 and set John McKenna the task of forming and managing the new team. McKenna, an Irishman, had contacts north of the border in Scotland and quickly set about putting together a team of Scotch Professors (see page 44).

Dubbed the 'team of Macs' they had their initial application to join the Football League turned down, and so they played their first season in the Lancashire League, romping home as champions (all right, they were equal on points with Blackpool, only champions on goal average, which was how it was done back in the day, and a single point ahead of third placed Bury, but the three of them were 10/11 points clear of the chasing pack which is pretty much a romp. It's just a romp with company).

And so, for the 1893/94 season, Liverpool, alongside Newcastle United, Rotherham Town and Woolwich Arsenal, took their place in the Second Division of the Football League.

★ THE FIRST TIME ★

Liverpool didn't stay long in the Second Division, going through the entire 1893/94 season unbeaten and emerging as champions, eight points clear of second placed Small Heath and 11 points clear of third placed Notts County. That's a romp in most people's books.

They failed to maintain their momentum in their first season in the top flight, and dropped back down to the Second Division for the next season – before rising back up as Second Division champions the next year. In 1896/97, they started to get their balance and achieved a creditable fifth place in the First Division, ninth the year after and then second in 1898/99, missing out on the title by two points.

They marked they start of the century with a 10th placed shrug, but then, in 1900/01, they became champions of England for the first of many times. Not bad, given that they'd only been formed eight years before. It took Chelsea 50 years to achieve the same feat.

It wasn't just the victory that was impressive, it was the way that it was achieved; it hinted at the legends that Liverpool would go on to provide. In February of the 1900/01 season, they were languishing in eighth place, nine points off the pace, but then, in March, against the odds and with an array of other clichés from the future ringing in their ears, they climbed the table, took the lead and delivered the title.

Their final game of the season was against the already relegated West Bromwich Albion, but, by all accounts, the Baggies gave a good account of themselves and the match was hard won. In a sign of the times, Liverpool FC returned home with their trophy by train and were met by a throng of people and a hastily assembled orchestra playing Georg Friedrich Handel's *See, the Conqu'ring Hero Comes!* (you know the one: *Daa daa de daa daa, da de da de da da daa, da de da de da da daa daa, da de daa da daaa*) before taking a horse-drawn carriage back to Anfield. Which all sounds terribly, terribly civilised. There were probably cucumber sandwiches being served somewhere.

★ RONNIE MORAN ★

Ronnie Moran joined Liverpool in 1949 and didn't retire from the club until 1998 – a 49-year career that saw him involved in bringing 44 trophies to Anfield. He clearly loved the place.

He joined the Liverpool set-up as a schoolboy in 1949, making his professional debut three years later as a defender and rising to become captain when Bill Shankly took over in 1959. He played a role in getting Liverpool out of the Second Division in 1961/62 before helping the team clinch the First Division title in 1963/64. He then also won the Charity Shield at the start of the next season.

He made 379 appearances in total, wearing the captain's armband 47 times while he was about it. He married one Saturday morning in spring 1957, and then helped Liverpool win that afternoon. History does not record how his wife took the news, but she probably had a pretty shrewd idea about where she stood in the marriage before she agreed to tie the knot.

As his playing days came to an end in 1966, he made the transition into management as a stalwart of Bill Shankly's Boot Room, alongside Reuben Bennett, Joe Fagan, Bob Paisley and Tom Saunders (they basically commandeered the Boot Room and used it as a place to congregate, have a cup of tea, have a natter about the Liverpool team and discuss ways of beating the next opposition).

He was there when Liverpool needed him, stepping up to be caretaker manager twice in the 1990s. He remained a vital part of the backroom staff until he retired in 1998, offering a consistent presence and playing a vital, and often vocal, role in steering numerous teams to phenomenal success over three decades.

BILLY LIDDELL'S RECORD OF SCORING FOR THE REDS IN 16 SUCCESSIVE SEASONS WAS FINALLY BEATEN BY STEVEN GERRARD IN 2014-15 – BUT LIDDELL'S RECORD HAD STOOD SINCE 1960.

"I WON A FEW THINGS
WITH THEM AND
HAD A LITTLE BIT OF
SUCCESS. YOU JUST
THINK, 'WELL, I'VE
DONE THAT, CAN I DO
IT AGAIN?'"

Ronnie Moran looks back at
a life in red.

CORMORANT OR SPOONBILL? SEAWEED ★ OR OLIVE BRANCH? ★

One of the most important things about Liverpool has been their commitment to consistency. Given that they have been – for long periods – one of the top English football teams, that consistency on the field can be difficult to maintain; however, off the field, they have retained a remarkable commitment to a handful of images and concepts.

One of these is the liver bird, a mythical beast that is said to represent Liverpool and has adorned Liverpool FC's crest since its inception.

A liver bird has been part of Liverpool's image as a city for a good long time. The origins are slightly obscure, but it is thought to date back to the 12th century when the collection of settlements on the banks of the Mersey was first granted its charter, which gave them certain rights in the eyes of the monarch (presumably this included the right to contribute to taxes).

As part of the deal, the nascent city's folk gained the right to use a common seal for official documents, and it appears that they chose a generic winged bird – possibly an eagle, maybe a dove – with a branch in its mouth that might have been from an olive tree – or possibly a sprig of broom (planta genista) – which could have been linked to King John's Plantagenet dynasty, since he was on the English throne at the time.

Fast-forward half a millennium and the generic winged bird – possibly an eagle, maybe a dove – had evolved into either a cormorant or possibly a spoonbill. The spoonbill is possible because the Dutch or German word for spoonbill is lever. 'Lever bird' becomes 'liver bird', which leads you to 'Liverpool', and everybody knows that folk in the Middle Ages loved a play on words. It could equally be a bit of a stretch, but it's worth noting that 500 years ago, you were quicker to get around the British Isles by coast than across land, and Liverpool would have been visited by sailors from all over Europe who might potentially have left a linguistic mark.

Either way, the item in the bird's mouth might have started out as an olive branch (which works if you think it's a dove), but has again changed down the years and is now generally accepted to be a frond of laver seaweed.

There is also a school of thought that suggests that Liverpool itself is named after a group of settlements that grew up around a body of water where laver seaweed was common, with 'laver pool' over time becoming 'Liverpool'. But then it could also have been that spoonbills, or 'lever birds', were common visitors and so it became 'Liverpool' that way.

Anyway, the bird was stylised and added to Liverpool's coat of arms in 1797 and hasn't really looked back (which is probably just as well because, if it did, it might realise that history is often (a) ambiguous, (b) bewildering and (c) gets in the way of the stuff about football).

'YOU'LL NEVER ★ WALK ALONE' ★

You'll Never Walk Alone was originally part of a Rodgers and Hammerstein musical that was first played in 1945, but in 1963, a local Liverpool band, Gerry and the Pacemakers, recorded a version and presented it as a single to Bill Shankly as a potential club anthem. He fell in love at first listen.

At the time, as Merseybeat was taking over the hit parade, the top 10 hits were played at Anfield in the run up to kick-off, and the Kopites would warm up their voices before the match by singing along. *You'll Never Walk Alone* was climbing the charts as the 1963 season got underway, reaching number one in October, but the Liverpool fans kept singing it even after it dropped out of the top 10.

By 1965, when it was being sung during the FA Cup final, it had become a regular refrain on the terraces. It's been sung in good times and bad ever since.

★ ROGER HUNT ★

Roger Hunt is still Liverpool's record league goal scorer, with 244 league goals and 285 in total during his 11 seasons at Anfield between 1958 and 1969. He won the First Division twice, lifted the FA Cup and won the Charity Shield for three consecutive years.

Hunt was one of the few Liverpool players to survive Bill Shankly's 1959 cull, which saw 24 players leave the club, and he scored 41 goals during the promotion-winning season of 1961/62. His goal against Arsenal was also the first to be shown on the inaugural edition of the BBC's *Match of the Day* programme at the start of the 1964/65 season.

Internationally, he went to the 1966 World cup and played in every game and scored three times, twice against France and once against Mexico. There are even those who suggest that, in the final, his quick and vocal celebration of Geoff Hurst's second goal, which might or might not have totally crossed the line, was what convinced the referee to notch it up. In total, he played for England 34 times, scoring 18 goals and was only on the losing side twice .

He came on as a substitute for what turned out to be his final match with Liverpool, scoring twice in two minutes. Always leave on a high.

·LIVERPOOL·

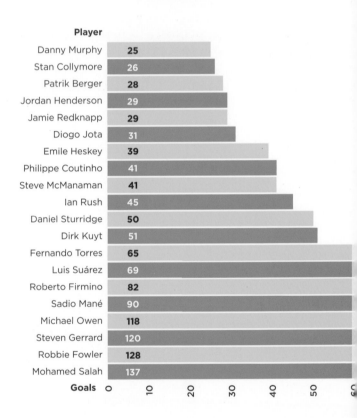

Player	Goals
Danny Murphy	25
Stan Collymore	26
Patrik Berger	28
Jordan Henderson	29
Jamie Redknapp	29
Diogo Jota	31
Emile Heskey	39
Philippe Coutinho	41
Steve McManaman	41
Ian Rush	45
Daniel Sturridge	50
Dirk Kuyt	51
Fernando Torres	65
Luis Suárez	69
Roberto Firmino	82
Sadio Mané	90
Michael Owen	118
Steven Gerrard	120
Robbie Fowler	128
Mohamed Salah	137

LIVERPOOL'S LEADING PREMIER LEAGUE ★ GOAL SCORERS ★

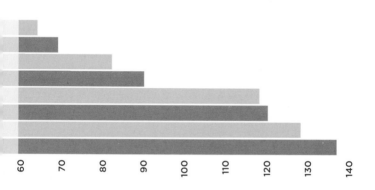

★ BOB PAISLEY ★

Stepping into Bill Shankly's shoes was never going to be easy (particularly given Shankly's tendency to show up at training sessions after his retirement), but Bob Paisley had been with the club for three-and-a-half decades when Shankly stepped down, so he could hit the ground running.

Paisley had signed his professional papers with Liverpool shortly before the outbreak of World War II so didn't make his debut as a player until the 1946/47 season – when Liverpool clinched the title by one point.

He made 277 total appearances for Liverpool and retired from playing in 1954 as Liverpool went down to the Second Division (they made a bad start to the season and never really recovered).

He then went through a period where he seems to have done lots of different things around Anfield, including both physiotherapist and brickie, building new dugouts and plumbing the Kemlyn Road toilets. It helps to have a trade.

When Shankly took over at Liverpool in 1959, he quickly recognised Paisley's potential, tactical nous and willingness to do whatever work was needed, so Shankly made Paisley an important part of the backroom staff. Fifteen years later, Shankly resigned after his victory in the 1974/75 FA Cup and, reluctantly, Paisley took over as manager.

What followed is the stuff of legend. Over the next 10 years, Liverpool won the First Division six times, coming second twice. There were six Charity Shields, three League Cups, a UEFA Cup, a UEFA Super Cup, and the small matter of three European Cups.

He retired at the end of the 1982/83 season, 44 years after he joined the club. Records that his teams set stand to this day, such as being the only manager to win the European Cup three times.

The club commemorated its most successful manager by putting up the Paisley Gateway and, later, a bronze statue of Paisley giving Emlyn Hughes a piggyback.

"IT'S NOT ABOUT THE LONG BALL OR THE SHORT BALL, IT'S ABOUT THE RIGHT BALL."

Bob Paisley proves his phenomenal understanding of the game.

THE OPPOSITION:
★ ARSENAL ★

Football's a funny old game. It's all about what happens during the 90 minutes on the pitch on any given Saturday afternoon – the incidents, the moments that drive a game forward until the ref blows up for the finish. Sometimes, there's a little bit of afters, but in terms of the football, it's actually quite a small period of time.

However, there's also the larger time period – the epoch

that a particular club is going through, and whether that aligns with something similar happening at the opposition. In the case of Liverpool and Arsenal, the wider context of club positions have been all-important.

Liverpool were the team of the 1980s, but it became clear that their glory days had faded in the mid-1990s – Arsenal were starting to stamp their authority on the game. It's the power of the Kop, but no matter how good the Liverpool team are at any given time, they can nearly always rise to an occasion – and in the mid-1990s, Liverpool vs Arsenal was always an occasion.

Looking a bit further back, though, Liverpool won every match they played against the then Woolwich Arsenal in the 19th century (all right, they only met four times, but that's still a 100% record).

When the pair met it was nearly always a high-scoring affair, with the first 0–0 not arriving until 1911, and fans having to wait a decade before they had to endure another. In total, the teams have drawn 63 times in the 239 times that they have played each other professionally. They've drawn around a quarter of the time, but at least there have been goals. Liverpool, meanwhile, have won 40% of the time.

Despite Arsenal's period of dominance in the mid-1990s to early 2000s, that tradition has continued into the Premier League, with Liverpool beating Arsenal around 45% of the time. The Anfield effect holds against Arsenal, with Liverpool winning more than half of their Premier League games at home but less than 30% away.

The tradition of very few 0–0 games has continued, with only five of their more than 60 Premier League meetings deflating to dreary no-score draws. In fact, on average, you are likely to see just under three goals when the two teams meet, which is pretty good in the big scheme of things.

LIVERPOOL HAS THE RECORD NUMBER OF RECOGNISED SUPPORTERS' CLUBS WITH OVER 100 OFFICIAL ORGANISATIONS IN 50 COUNTRIES AROUND THE WORLD.

"SOMETIMES I FEEL I'M HARDLY WANTED IN THIS LIVERPOOL TEAM. IF I GET TWO OR THREE SAVES TO MAKE, I'VE HAD A BUSY DAY."

Ray Clemence delivers a masterclass in the gentle art of the humblebrag.

★ IAN CALLAGHAN ★

42

Ian Callaghan was Liverpool born and bred; he spent the best part of two decades with the Reds, making 640 league appearances and 857 appearances in all competitions. Basically, he bossed the midfield from 1960 to 1978.

He joined as an apprentice but quickly made the breakthrough into the first team as Liverpool got themselves out of the Second Division at the end of the 1961/62 season. He was a mainstay of the phenomenally successful teams of the 1960s and 1970s under Bill Shankly and Bob Paisley.

Callaghan played for England four times and was part of the squad for the 1966 World Cup victory, although he didn't play in the final itself. The 11-year and 49-day gap between playing in the group stages in 1966 and his appearance against Switzerland in 1977 is the longest gap between appearances for a player in the English national squad. It also means that he was the final member of the 1966 squad to play a competitive match for England.

Although only booked once in his entire career, Callaghan said that he 'had got away with murder' at times, and would have been booked every week if he played in today's game.

RAISING A GLASS TO THE SCOTCH ★ PROFESSORS ★

The world of 19th-century football sounds chaotic. Rules came and went, teams were formed, arguments happened, teams broke apart and moved to other places ...

One of the biggest debates in the sport revolved around amateurism vs professionalism. For some, all sport should be amateur, something that gentlemen did at the weekend, with matches interrupted for light sherries and always played in the best spirit. In the working-class towns of the north of England, there was an appreciation of how much better a game could become if the players were professional.

So, although association football might have been born in south London, it was raised in the north. People wanted a spectacle on a Saturday afternoon, even if they couldn't play; what they wanted was something to see, rather than a handful of people in nice jerseys being terribly nice to one another. High stakes and grit with your fish, chips and bits.

As a result, the English authorities started to grudgingly move towards professionalism and accepting that footballers deserved to be paid.

Scotland, meanwhile, was slower on the uptake – and paying sportspeople remained illegal. At the same time, though, the Scottish game developed slightly differently. In England in the 1880s, people were appreciated for their fine dribbling skills, but north of the border, probably because pitches were so often waterlogged from the endless rain, players were more likely to pass the ball because it was easier to move it through the air than across the land.

And while plenty of people in England were exceptionally sniffy about the way that the Scots played the game, in four of the five internationals that were held between 1878 and 1882, Scotland beat England 7–2, 5–4, 6–1 and 5–1. You might not like it, but passing worked.

So, what you ended up with was a situation where there

were Scottish players looking to make money off their abilities and innovative approach to the sport, and English teams that were willing to pay players that could help them up their game. These so-called 'Scotch Professors' (who may or may not have had a liking for Scotch, but were certainly Scots) became a prominent feature of the English game in the 1880s and early 1890s.

The newly formed Liverpool FC in 1892 was known as the 'team of Macs' because of its initial reliance on Scottish players. This started a relationship between Liverpool FC and Scotland that has lasted to this day.

Why were they known as the 'Scotch Professors' rather than the 'Scots Professors'? Drammed if anyone knows!

BOB PAISLEY WON 31 TROPHIES AT ANFIELD AS PLAYER, COACH AND MANAGER.

"I'VE BEEN HERE DURING THE BAD TIMES TOO. ONE YEAR WE CAME SECOND."

Bob Paisley reflects on the 'tough' times of his glorious Anfield reign.

★ RON YEATS ★

What do you look for in a central defender? 6 foot 2 inches high and solidly built is a good place to start – so far as Bill Shankly was concerned, and he signed Ron Yeats in 1961 from Dundee United and almost immediately made him Liverpool's captain.

Over the next decade, Yeats played 454 games in all competitions for Liverpool, 358 of them in the league, and he was Liverpool's longest-serving captain until Steven Gerrard came along. He was captain when Liverpool finally got their hands on the FA Cup in the pouring rain at the end of the 1964/65 season, apparently telling Queen Elizabeth II that he was absolutely knackered before remembering who he was talking to. She was, apparently, amused and sympathetic in a regal sort of way.

Yeats is the 'Big Ron' that Everton fans so warmly remember when they sing their light-hearted comedy song, *The Banks of the Royal Blue Mersey*.

★ ANFIELD ★

Anfield is an important character in the Liverpool story. It's not the biggest stadium in the country, it's not the swankiest, but it is full of character and is home, and sometimes a fortress, for Liverpool. There have been discussions about moving to other venues, but they've never really got very far. There's too much heritage.

Anfield's stands had been built to welcome 8,000 spectators during the previous tenant's tenure, but the stadium is estimated to have had the capacity for 20,000 in the late 1890s.

In 1895, Archibald Leitch, who pretty much had a British monopoly on stadium design for the first few decades of the 20th century, added a new stand on the site of the current Main Stand. It's funny to think these days – when people complain that modern stadiums are all identikit and corporate and look like a flying saucer has beamed down from on high – that in the period between the 1890s and his death at the end of the 1930s, Leitch was involved in the design of virtually every football stadium in Britain, as well as a fair few of the rugby, cricket and hockey venues.

He was involved in the development or redevelopment of more than 30 stadiums across Britain, often delivering similar projects for teams within a few miles of each other, including both Anfield and Goodison Park. If you think stadiums are all the same today, you should have seen what they were like in the 1930s.

Either way, since then the improvements at Anfield have been gradual, neatly avoiding the risk that teams like Chelsea have faced when undergoing major, expensive projects and being caught out by economic changes at the worst possible moment. Building or redeveloping a stadium is a long-term project with a lot of short-term risk, and it's not something to get into without a decent amount of cash behind you.

While a move away from Anfield has been suggested on occasion, aside from a few plans here and there, nothing has ever materialised, and Liverpool and Anfield continue their long and happy association.

Liverpool have been at Anfield for more than 130 years so, unsurprisingly, there are a string of stats that tell a tale, but there are two that are worth contemplating. There are 11 seasons where Liverpool did not lose a league match at Anfield, specifically the 1893/94, 1970/71, 1976/77, 1978/79, 1979/80, 1987/88, 2008/09, 2017/18, 2018/19, 2019/20 and 2021/22 seasons.

At the same time, Liverpool's longest run of matches without a win at Anfield in its history took place in 2020/21, during the Covid-19 lockdowns that meant all matches were being played behind closed doors.

Does this suggest that there's something in the air at Anfield that offers Liverpool teams a very real level of support? Maybe, although it's not true that the crowd at the Kop can suck the ball into the goal … probably.

"I DON'T LIKE CHAMPAGNE, DON'T SMOKE CIGARS, HAVEN'T ANY REAL JEWELLERY AT ALL APART FROM THE EIGHT PIECES OF GOLD I PICKED UP AT ANFIELD. THE MOST IMPORTANT RELATIONSHIP AT A FOOTBALL CLUB IS NOT BETWEEN THE MANAGER AND CHAIRMAN, BUT THE PLAYERS AND THE FANS."

John Toshack is fairly calm about the trinkets he picked up here and there.

★ IAN ST JOHN ★

Ian St John was pivotal to Shankly's team in the 1960s. He signed from his native Motherwell, with the story going that the Liverpool board was reluctant to splash out the £37,500 required for his signature. Bill Shankly cut through their objections, suggesting that the club couldn't afford *not* to buy him.

He lived up to the promise, announcing his arrival with a hat-trick against Everton (Liverpool lost the match, so don't dwell on it – focus on the hat-trick). After seven years languishing in the Second Division, St John gave the Liverpool team a cutting edge and they emerged from the Second Division in 1961/62 as champions eight points clear of the pack. A romp.

They came eighth the next year, but in 1963/64 came racing up the outside once again and took the First Division title from holders Everton (who came third).

The 1960s was a very physical time in football, but St John held his own, once flattening Fulham's Mark Pearson with an impressive right, right, left combination after the Fulham man had pulled his hair. He walked straight to the dressing room without stopping to hear what the referee thought about it.

St John spent a decade at Liverpool, winning the Second Division once in 1961/62, the First Division twice in 1963/64 and 1965/66, the FA Cup in 1964/65 and the Charity Shield in three successive years – in 1964, 1965 and 1966. He made 336 league appearances, finding the net 95 times, and played 21 times for Scotland.

After moving on from Liverpool, he played for a couple of other teams, went into management for a few years and then into punditry, ultimately forming a partnership with Jimmy Greaves and hosting *Saint and Greavsie*. The show was cancelled when Sky took over the football broadcasting rights and the Premier League was created.

LIVERPOOL HAS NEVER WON THE LEAGUE WITHOUT A SCOTTISH PLAYER ON THE TEAM.

"THERE IS NO ONE ANYWHERE IN THE WORLD AT ANY STAGE WHO IS ANY BIGGER OR ANY BETTER THAN THIS FOOTBALL CLUB."

Kenny Dalglish keeps it simple.

THE STORY OF
★ THE KOP ★

The Kop at Anfield is one of the most famous celebrated places in world football. Performing in front of the Kop in a Liverpool shirt is probably something that every football player dreams of, even if they'd never admit it in public. It is one of football's sacred grounds.

Anfield's Kop is not the only one in English football (and there are a few in other sports as well); it's not even the first (that honour belongs to a long-forgotten south London team called Woolwich Arsenal, whose Manor Ground also had a steep hill for fans to stand on that was known as 'the Kop'), but it is undoubtedly the most famous. There are a couple of reasons for this.

The Kop is named after Spion Kop hill in South Africa, the site of a fierce battle during the Second Boer War in 1900. The British were attempting to relieve their forces that were under siege at nearby Ladysmith. It's a long and fascinating story, but the long and short of it is that the

British had the numbers, the Boers had modern equipment and were well entrenched. The British attack was badly co-ordinated, and the soldiers, many of whom were from Lancashire and Liverpool, suffered significant losses as a result (it's been suggested that there may have been a certain amount of intransigence among the officer classes of the day).

Drawing a veil over that, the Kop stand at Anfield was built to celebrate Liverpool winning their second league title in 1905. It was already the place where the most ardent fans congregated, but when a roof was added in 1928, the acoustics meant that the noise generated by the Kop was reflected back on to the pitch, making it a fairly awesome – and pretty intimidating – place to come.

The Kop was redeveloped in the early 1990s after the Taylor Report recommended all-seater stadiums, but it is still a bastion of Liverpool support, and Liverpool players adore playing in front of it. Most other players find it terrifying.

★ UP THE FLAGPOLE ★

Isambard Kingdom Brunel was a towering figure in Britain's Industrial Revolution, designing and building the tools and architecture that helped move the country from its agrarian roots to its modern destiny (that's what it says in this brochure anyway). He built the first tunnels under navigable rivers, he built bridges, shipyards and railways.

He also built three ships, the third of which, the SS Great Eastern, was the largest ship ever built at the time. It was designed to take 4,000 passengers – in varying degrees of luxury – from England to Australia with a single load of coal because it was believed when she was ordered in the 1850s that there wasn't any coal down under. By the time she was launched, coal had been found, which changed the economics of operating a massive ship with extensive coal storage. So she was converted to take people to and from America instead.

The ship did many things during her working career, including laying the first transatlantic cables between

Britain and the US to make instant communication between the two countries possible for the first time.

She was a marvel of engineering, but she was a big ship with significant running costs, was expensive to repair and very unwieldy. She is said to have been responsible for sinking at least 10 ships by accidentally ramming them. This meant that she had a much shorter working life than investors originally hoped.

Towards the end of her days, the Great Eastern was used as a floating billboard, sailing up and down the Mersey advertising Liverpool's famous Lewis's department store. Then, in 1886, she struck and sunk one of the tugs that was helping manoeuvre her to the Liverpool Exhibition. Two years later, she was sold for scrap.

So what? Well, in the 1890s there was a need for a new flagpole for Anfield and someone decided that it would be good to use the topmast of the SS Great Eastern. It stands at the Kop to this day.

★ EMLYN HUGHES ★

According to Bill Shankly, Emlyn Hughes had everything that a footballer needed: ability, guts, speed, good in the air. And while we'd never go against the great man's analysis, there is one thing that he didn't mention: enthusiasm. Hughes genuinely seemed to love what he was doing.

Known affectionately as 'Crazy horse' as a result of his galloping runs up and down the pitch, it's sometimes easy to miss quite how good he was at finding himself the right place to be in. Whether it was to hammer home a deflected shot, cut a defence apart with a measured 1–2, or simply walloping the ball into the back of the net from outside the penalty area, he was nearly always in the right place at the right time. He might have looked like a crazy horse as he charged up and down the pitch, but it was effective.

He joined Liverpool in 1967, staying at Anfield for 12 years and making 474 league appearances. He also received 62 England caps between 1969 and 1980, taking the captain's armband when Bobby Moore ended his time with the Three Lions.

★ THIS IS ANFIELD ★

It was a groundsman that had the bright idea. He suggested putting up a sign in the players' tunnel saying 'Welcome to Anfield' as a way of reminding the opposition where they were and who they were playing. The idea reached Bill Shankly, who finessed it. The sign shouldn't read 'Welcome to Anfield'. The opposition should never feel welcome. The sign should be a statement: This is Anfield.

And so the sign was put up at the end of the players' tunnel leading out on to the turf.

There have actually been three versions of the sign used down the years, although the version that's currently on display is the second version.

The version put up by Shankly was replaced in 1974 when Bob Paisley took over. This first version is now said to be enjoying a lengthy retirement hanging behind a bar at a bed and breakfast on the Isle of Man.

The replacement held its place for 24 of the most glorious years in Liverpool's history, overseeing the tunnel as the team took 10 league titles, five League Cups, four European Cups, three FA Cups, a UEFA Cup and a Super Cup. Which amounts to a trophy a season.

This second version was taken down in 1998, as Liverpool's light had started to dim a bit (relatively). The third version was in place for 14 years, and only witnessed two FA Cups, three Football League Cups, two Charity Shields, one European Cup, one Europa League Cup and two UEFA Super Cups. For most teams that would be deemed a relatively successful period, but this is Liverpool ...

When Brendan Rodgers took over as Liverpool manager in 2012, he stumbled across the second version of the sign in a store cupboard and set about having it put back in place. He reasoned that if a little of its magic could rub off on his players, it would help elevate Liverpool back to the heights of the 1970s and 1980s.

It wasn't quite to be, but when his successor, Jürgen Klopp, took over, he bought into the magic and banned his players from touching the sign until they'd brought some silverware back to Anfield. It was four years before the team lifted the Champion's League trophy but then they took the Premier League a year later and there was no doubt that that crop of players had earned the right to touch the sign.

Since 2012, the sign has witnessed an FA Cup, an EFL Cup, a Charity Shield, a UEFA Champions League, a UEFA Super Cup, a FIFA Club World Cup and, most importantly, that elusive Premier League title.

Whichever version is used, the 'This is Anfield' sign has achieved legendary status, and there are said to be dire consequences for any opposition player that is caught touching the sign. Arsenal's Ian Wright claims to have done the deed, but he did it while the teams were warming up and no one was looking. The fact that Wright didn't say which match that he'd touched the sign before suggests that it didn't end well for Arsenal.

Manchester United's Wout Weghorst went a step further and touched the sign as the players made their way out on to the pitch. He claims he was trying to wind up fellow Dutch international Virgil van Dijk. The incident took place on Sunday 5 March 2023, and United came back through the tunnel 105 minutes later having been walloped 7-0. Anyone else want to risk it?

"I FELT THE POWER OF ANFIELD, IT WAS MAGNIFICENT."

José Mourinho reminds the world that he's not always negative.

★ KEVIN KEEGAN ★

Kevin Keegan was the poster boy for Liverpool's success in the 1970s. Joining in 1971 from Fourth Division's Scunthorpe United, Keegan quickly made himself an Anfield favourite by scoring 12 minutes into his debut against Nottingham Forest. This was despite turning up half an hour late for the pre-match because he hadn't realised what match-day traffic would be like around Anfield.

He started out as a midfielder but was quickly moved to the front, initially alongside John Toshack, as his competitive nature and high levels of fitness enabled him to harry defenders throughout a game. He was trialled up front during a youth game, scoring four of the seven goals in a 7–0 rout.

Keegan made 230 league appearances for Liverpool, knocking in 68 goals, and, occasionally, trying to knock out an opposition player or two. During his time at Anfield, he won the First Division three times in 1972/73, 1975/76, 1976/77, the FA Cup in 1973/74, the FA Charity Shield twice in 1974 and 1976, the European Cup in 1976/77 and the UEFA Cup in both 1972/73 and 1975/76. He also won 63 caps for England, scoring 21 goals. Quite impressive for a kid who feared he might struggle a bit if he went up to First Division football.

He was almost as famous for his hairstyle as he was for his football. Up until Keegan, footballers had only really come in two flavours: hairy or neat. Keegan's bubble perm showed that it was possible to be both. He made it okay for players to express their freedom and individuality through hairstyles and opened the door to so many of the fantastic styles that we see on today's football pitches. So, yeah, thanks for that.

He also had a (thankfully) brief stab at pop stardom, but that was after he'd left Liverpool – so we really don't need to think too much about it. His one single was a moderate success in Germany.

"BOSS WOULDN'T LET US TOUCH THE SIGN UNTIL WE WON A TROPHY … NOW IS THE TIME."

Gini Wijnaldum joins a pantheon of Liverpool legends.

THE OPPOSITION:
★ TOTTENHAM HOTSPUR ★

Tottenham Hotspur: everyone loves a tryer. The two teams have been competing for more than a century, and Liverpool have beaten them on just under half of their meetings. It's usually a fairly healthy rivalry, with Spurs repeatedly getting themselves close to silverware but never quite getting over the final hurdle. Underestimate them at your peril, though, they did once put seven past Liverpool, although that was in 1963 and Liverpool has put seven past them twice (in 1914 and 1978).

The two teams have had some great games down the years, but there's not a great deal of beef between them. Most of the time, they show up, do what they need to do, and move on to other things without much of a backwards glance.

Focusing on the Premier League years, Liverpool have continued to win just under half of the time, but proof of how powerful the Kop can be, they've won nearly two-thirds of their games at home against Tottenham and drawn around a third. What this means is that they lose to Tottenham at Anfield less than 10% of the time (it's 7% if you want to be pedantic, but we're trying to keep things fairly general).

Whether it's at Anfield or one of the Tottenham grounds, you get a fairly decent return for your ticket, with an average of nearly three goals per match . There have been nine games in the Premier League with four or more goals, which is not bad, but, statistically, they are just not quite as good as the other north London team.

All that said, given that in recent seasons Liverpool have tended to have to accept that the biggest prize they are going to get is a top four finish and the promise of Champions League football, winning against Tottenham, who tend to be in a similar position, is always important.

★ HEYSEL ★

In May 1985, Liverpool had reached the European Cup final for the second year in a row and were facing Juventus at the Heysel Stadium in Belgium. The two teams had come up against one another other in a tense European Super Cup encounter five months earlier and there was little love lost between the two sets of fans. There had also been ugly scenes at the end of the previous year's European Cup final which Liverpool won after a penalty shootout, when Roma fans had set upon the visiting Liverpool fans, pelting them with missiles.

Heysel Stadium was also in a sorry state, with inadequate barriers, dubious seat allocations and crumbling walls. Concerns had been raised about the facilities before the match, but the authorities made the decision to carry on.

An hour before the match, the two sets of fans were trading insults and throwing missiles at each other, and then at 7pm local time, a group of Liverpool fans broke through the chicken wire barrier that had been put up between two of the sections. They rushed into a section of neutral and Juventus fans that included several children and in the pandemonium that followed, one of the stadium's internal walls collapsed.

39 people were crushed, the youngest of whom was 11 years old.

There are plenty of reasons why the tragedy occurred, but the blame was placed firmly at the feet of the Liverpool's fans, a symptom of English football terraces being populated by yobs and hooligans. UEFA placed an indefinite ban all English clubs from European competitions, a ruling that lasted for five years for the majority of clubs, with Liverpool serving an extra year.

There is no excuse for what happened, but the violence that the Liverpool fans had faced previously and the disrepair that the Heysel Stadium was known to be in before the match combined to turn a potential for incident into a likelihood. Most people now agree that putting the blame solely on the Liverpool fans was unfair.

★ THE SPICE BOYS ★

Sometimes football becomes part of the social fabric of the nation, bringing everyone together, united, to scratch their heads and say "huh, how did we get to this?"

One such moment came in the 1990s, with the emergence of the Spice Boys, a group of Liverpool players, or perhaps playaz, who became key fixtures of the celebrity gossip pages as they committed the cardinal sin of being younger, fitter, (mostly) prettier and (generally) better dressed than the majority of the rest of us. The press took to calling them the Spice Boys because the Spice Girls were a popular beat combo at the time, and there was a rumour that a Liverpool player had been seen out on the tiles with a Spice Girl.

It was the Liverpool team's decision to wear matching cream Armani suits on their way into the 1996 FA Cup final that seemed to be the "moment" that people started discussing it all. The fact that Liverpool didn't win added to the debate, particularly when it was followed shortly after by the England team drinking and getting up to "high jinks" in the famed dentist's chair incident as they were supposed to be preparing for Euro 96 (nightclub, plus dentist's chair, plus copious bottles of booze equals sore heads and unfavourable headlines). Perhaps, the finger waggers said, if footballers focused on the football rather than cavorting in nightclubs, England might not have gone out on penalties. Again.

The thing is though, football had always had a heavy drinking culture. There's a very long and very sad list of exceptional talent that was lost to off-field distractions that stretched back for a century. It could be that the debate around the Spice Boys, whether the criticism of them was justified or not, enabled managers to put more pressure on players to become more professional and call time on the drinking culture.

It's also not impossible that the whole thing marked the beginning of the end for the tradition of the FA Cup song, with managers starting to enforce more focus on the football rather than the peripheral stuff. Which is a shame, because 1986's *Sitting on Top of the World* by the Liverpool team is, as the kids say, a stonewall banga of a choon that Bill Shankly would have absolutely adored. Why it was never put forward for Eurovision is a mystery.

★ ALAN HANSEN ★

Alan Hansen gave up on football at 15 to concentrate on becoming a professional golfer. It was two years before his family managed to convince him to try out for Hibernian, and even then he turned down their offer of a professional contract. He was in the crowd when his brother lifted the Scottish League Cup with Partick Thistle in 1971, though, and it could have been that experience that proved to him there was more fun to be had on the pitch than on the greens.

He ended up joining Partick himself, working with his brother to help get them up to the Scottish First Division and enjoy a creditable fifth place the year after. He was sold to Liverpool for the 1977/78 season, the deal agreed before the end of the previous season, so he could once against watch from the terraces as his future team clinched both the English First Division title and the European Cup.

He didn't have to watch for long, though, as he went on to enjoy eight First Division titles in 1978/79, 1979/80, 1981/82, 1982/83, 1983/84, 1985/86, 1987/88 and 1989/90, two FA Cups in 1985/86 and 1988/89, four League Cups in consecutive years in 1980/81, 1981/82, 1982/83 and 1983/84, six FA Charity Shields in 1977 (shared), 1979, 1980, 1982, 1986 (shared) and 1989, a Football League Super

Cup in 1986, three European Cups in 1977/78, 1980/81 and 1983/84 and a UEFA Super Cup in 1977.

He made 620 appearances for Liverpool, scoring 14 goals; almost as importantly, he helped build a dynasty of Liverpool defenders around him that took the club to the very top of world football.

Not bad for a second-choice career.

THE FIRST LIVERPOOL FOOTBALL CLUB WAS FORMED IN 1857. THEY PLAYED RUGBY UNION AND WERE EVENTUALLY AMALGAMATED WITH ST HELENS RUFC.

"THE MOTTO 'THIS IS ANFIELD' IS NO MARKETING SPIN. THERE'S SOMETHING ABOUT IT THAT YOU WILL FIND IN NO OTHER STADIUM IN THE WORLD."

Pep Guardiola gives respect where it's due.

ARSENAL AND TOTTENHAM HATE EACH OTHER BECAUSE OF LIVERPOOL AND ★ MANCHESTER UNITED ★

Arsenal and Tottenham were probably always going to be on a collision course once Arsenal made the decision to move from Woolwich in south London to within a couple of miles of Tottenham in north London. It's different in Liverpool because there aren't any other big teams nearby, but elsewhere in the country, having two big teams in close proximity never fails to cause tension. There was always likely to be a spark.

That spark came in 1919 when Arsenal were voted into the First Division at the expense of Spurs, at least in the analysis of the folk from White Hart Lane. The rights and wrongs of this are not really an issue for a book about Liverpool Football Club, but, if we are honest, you don't have to look too hard to see how Liverpool and Manchester United might just have had quite a lot to do with causing the issue.

In 1915, several players from Liverpool and Manchester United were caught up in a match-fixing scandal. It was an ugly business and there were red faces all round, but the upshot was that at the end of the season, with two relegation places at the time, Manchester United had 30 points, Chelsea 29 and Spurs 28, so the two London teams were going to be relegated with Manchester United escaping the drop by a single point. If there hadn't been any match-fixing, Spurs would still have been demoted, but Chelsea would have escaped and Manchester United would, instead, have faced the ignominy of the drop.

A total of seven players – four Liverpool, three Manchester United – were thought to have conspired to fix the match in question, but the motivation was found to be financial rather than an attempt to skew the league, and the teams themselves weren't implicated. As a result, the players were banned but the teams weren't docked points. From the sounds of things, the players in question are simply thought to have looked at the 7/1 odds on a 2–0 Manchester United victory, factored in the tensions in Europe at the time, realised that they were probably going to be called up, and thought they might as well go for a big pay day.

Four years later, football was due to resume after World War I based on the league positions from the end of the 1915 season, but the First Division was going to be extended with two extra teams coming up from the Second Division, in addition to the two teams that would have been promoted normally (in this case, Second Division champions Derby and second-placed Preston North End).

The additional two places were to be decided by a vote. In the first vote, Chelsea were given unanimous support to come straight back into the First Division because everyone felt guilty about them potentially going down because of the actions of a handful of dodgy individuals.

The vote for the second place comes up and it's Arsenal that get the nod rather than Spurs. Some say it was the result of Arsenal putting the blag in and some say it was just the way that things were done and there wasn't anything particularly untoward about the whole thing. The bottom line, though, is that Chelsea stayed up and were joined by Arsenal, Tottenham went down, White Hart Lane's resident parrot dropped dead and the phrase 'sick as a parrot' is said to have been born.

Liverpool and Manchester United probably shouldn't feel too guilty; the chances are the two north London teams were always going to end up in a row, but it's never nice to be part of something that leads to two friends falling out.

THE LAST PLAYER TO MOVE DIRECTLY FROM LIVERPOOL TO MANCHESTER UNITED OR VICE VERSA WAS PHIL CHISNALL IN 1964.

THE RISING OF
★ THE LIVER ★

The Royal Liver Building overlooking the Mersey has two of the most famous liver birds nesting on top of it. Do they have big, grand names as befit these mighty avian protectors of the Mersey? No, they are called Bertie and Bella, which is fine, but you can't help but feel that Liverpool is slightly taking the mickey. Put it like this, if they were in London, they'd be called something like Erasmus the Unconquered and Ermintrude the Redoubtable. But no, Bertie and Bella it is.

Bella is looking out to sea to keep an eye out for the city's seafarers; Bertie is looking back into the city to keep a watchful eye on the seafarers' waiting families. Although some suggest he's making sure that the pubs open on time.

They arrived in 1911 when the Royal Liver Building was built and have resolutely had their backs to each other ever since. It is said that if they ever look upon each other then they would mate, fly away, the Mersey would flood and Liverpool would cease to exist.

There are said to be approximately one hundred liver birds dotted around the city, mostly perched on top of lamp posts in the centre of town, but also roosting on municipal buildings and dotted throughout various designs around the place. When you've got something that works, and is uniquely yours, you should make the most of it.

It's never been definitively stated which liver bird adorns the crest of Liverpool FC, possibly because if it did become clear that it was Bella or Bertie, the other one would fly away in a huff, Anfield would be flooded and Liverpool FC would cease to exist.

LIVERPOOL ONLY CONCEDED 16 GOALS IN THE 42 GAMES OF THE 1978/79 LEAGUE SEASON.

★ KENNY DALGLISH ★

Kenny Dalglish spent more than a decade as a player for Liverpool, galvanising the team into a period of success that led to him being known as King Kenny.

He joined from Celtic in 1977, continuing a long and healthy tradition of Scottish players travelling south to delight the Anfield crowds (see page 44). During his time with Liverpool, he won six English League championships, the FA Cup, four League Cups, five FA Charity Shields, three European Cups and one European Super Cup.

When Joe Fagan retired at the end of the 1984/85 season following the Heysel Stadium disaster, Dalglish took on the player-manager role. He continued Liverpool's success by nurturing younger players and increasingly only pulled on his boots when he was really needed. He continued to manage the team to success but retired in 1991 after the Hillsborough tragedy.

He returned to the club as caretaker and then permanent manager between 2011 and 2012 and has maintained ties with the club ever since.

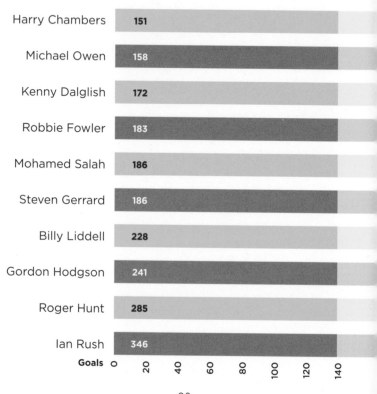

	Goals
Harry Chambers	151
Michael Owen	158
Kenny Dalglish	172
Robbie Fowler	183
Mohamed Salah	186
Steven Gerrard	186
Billy Liddell	228
Gordon Hodgson	241
Roger Hunt	285
Ian Rush	346

LIVERPOOL'S LEADING ALL-TIME ★ GOAL SCORERS ★

(ALL COMPETITIONS)

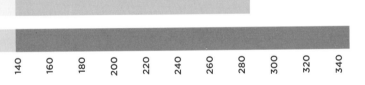

140 160 180 200 220 240 260 280 300 320 340 360

★ RESPECT THE BADGE ★

So the time came when Liverpool FC needed to come up with a visual identity, and frankly it didn't really take very long. For the first 50 or so years of the club's history, it used a version of the city of Liverpool's coat of arms, which is basically a liver bird flanked by Neptune, Roman god of water and the sea, and Triton, Greek god of the sea. Because, as a general rule, the more gods you have on your side, the better – particularly if you are a mythical bird, such as the liver, that doesn't actually seem to have any magical powers other than the ability to mooch into the history books through some sort of mystical mist of time.

In the team's original crest, the motto of the city of Liverpool, *Deus nobis haec otia fecit* which translates to something along the lines of 'God has given us this blessing', was placed at the top of the badge and the words 'Liverpool Football Club' were contained in a scroll at the bottom.

It was changed in the early 1950s, seemingly when Liverpool City Council objected to Liverpool FC using the crest of the city on the grounds that a couple of their citizens might conceivably have supported Everton. Seems unlikely, but there it is.

So Liverpool pared the crest right back to the most important element – the liver bird – which it had been using on things like flags for many years (presumably because it was a lot easier to sew).

The bird has been redrawn a few times, sometimes in silhouette, sometimes with full plumage. It has also been shown within various different shields, and the basic shield has been embellished with the Shankly Gates and the eternal flames in memory of the victims of the Heysel and Hillsborough disasters, but overall it's been fairly similar since the mid-1970s.

Simply, instantly recognisable Liverpool.

★ GRAEME SOUNESS ★

Graeme Souness joined Liverpool from Middlesbrough and quickly ingratiated himself with the Anfield faithful by scoring on his debut against Manchester United, a goal that was later voted as fans' goal of the season. He joined at the same time as Kenny Dalglish and Alan Hansen, as Bob Paisley looked to shore up his team after the European Cup victory in 1977.

As a strategy, it's probably fair to say that it worked out, with Liverpool retaining the European Cup in 1978 and winning the English Football League in both 1978/79 and 1979/80 – and then three consecutive times in 1981/82, 1982/83 and 1983/84. The team also won the Football League Cup four consecutive times in 1980/81, 1981/82, 1982/83, 1983/84, and the Charity Shield in 1979, 1980 and 1982. They also won the European Cup twice more for good measure in 1980/81 and 1983/84.

Souness left Liverpool in 1984 but returned as manager between 1991 and 1994 when Kenny Dalglish stepped away from the role. During this time, he brought through some prodigious talent, including Robbie Fowler, Steve McManaman and Jamie Redknapp.

★ STEPS: BACK TO YOU ★

The footballing authorities don't go out of their way to get things wrong, but sometimes it just happens; they stay committed to a rule and try to make it work rather than tearing it up, going back to the drawing board and working out an alternative that is quicker, easier and much less hassle.

Let's take you back to the 1960s. Football ages differently to people (it's a sport, so why wouldn't it?), so at this point it had kind of reached its metaphorical teenage years. It knew what it was, it was well on the way to delivering its potential, but it still had a whole lot to learn.

It was felt that, in some situations, some teams were starting to waste time by passing back to the goalie, who would then pick up the ball and mooch about for a while and run the clock down. It wasn't illegal and, to be fair, game management has always been a key component to winning. But it slowed the game right down and encouraged teams to protect a 1–0 lead.

So, the governing bodies of football, in their infinite wisdom, decided to introduce the steps rule. Goalies could only take four steps with the ball before having to do something else with it, which seemed like a good way of speeding the game up.

Except the rules weren't very well written, and football has as many clever buggers as any other walk of life, so we ended up with a situation where goalies received the ball, picked it up, took a couple of steps, put it down again, dribbled for a bit, picked it back up, took another couple of steps, thought for a bit, put it down ... There was nothing illegal in this, according to a strict interpretation of the wording of the rules, but it hardly encouraged fast, flowing football.

There were tweaks and changes to the wording and people kept finding ways around the rules until, one day in the early 1990s, someone had the bright idea of simply banning the pass back, which put an end to all kinds of shenanigans overnight. Yes, it's true! The introduction of the pass-back rule meant that there has not been a single shenanigan committed on the football pitch since 1992.

One of the final pass backs in the history of top-level English football took place in the dying moments of the FA Cup Final in 1991/92 at Wembley between Liverpool and Sunderland. Liverpool were 2-0 up and cruising to victory when Steve Nicol nudged the ball back to Bruce Grobelaar, who clasped the ball lovingly to his chest. The goalkeeper paused to look around ruefully, perhaps taking a moment to appreciate the historical significance of his actions … or perhaps just killing off a few more precious seconds of the game.

These days, technically, goalkeepers are not allowed to hold the ball for more than six seconds after they have caught it in open play.

So, between the pass-back rule and the six-second hold rule, the game has become much faster. And people can focus on the game, rather than trying to keep count of the steps that a goalie has taken. The goalie is still not supposed to take more than four steps with the ball, but it's less of an issue as a result of the pass-back rule.

"I BELIEVE A YOUNG PLAYER WILL RUN THROUGH A BARBED WIRE FENCE FOR YOU. AN OLDER PLAYER LOOKS FOR A HOLE IN THE FENCE."

Brendan Rodgers neatly shows how management had evolved since Shankly's time.

★ HILLSBOROUGH ★

One of the worst disasters in modern British sporting history took place in April 1989. 94 people died and 766 people were injured during a crush before an FA Cup semi-final between Liverpool and Nottingham Forest at Sheffield's Hillsborough Stadium. Three further people succumbed to their injuries after the event.

There were many factors that contributed to the tragedy. There were fewer trains than normal to take people to the match. This forced fans to drive to Sheffield, but roadworks on the M62 delayed many journeys, and Liverpool fans didn't arrive until just before the match. Meanwhile, for a variety of reasons, the police leadership team on the day was very inexperienced and had never managed a sporting event on the scale of an FA Cup semi-final. The physical geography of the stadium also meant that Liverpool's fans were allocated the smaller of its two ends. This was arranged so that the two sets of fans would not cross each other's paths on their way in, but it also meant that large numbers of Liverpool fans trying to get through a smaller number of turnstiles. These factors combined to create a crush that left nearly 100 people dead.

There are two aspects to the tragedy that need to be acknowledged. Firstly, the loss of life didn't need to happen. There had been previous incidents at the stadium that pointed to a significant risk, and the people organising the fixture and in control on the day could have made better decisions before the crush.

The second aspect of the tragedy though – the attempts by the authorities to cover up what really happened and the collusion by certain sections of the British media that decided to take their stories at face value – was frankly appalling. The fact that it took nearly a quarter of a century for the state to accept what it had put the families of the victims through is a shameful reflection on Britain's reputation for decency and fair play.

Lessons were learned from both the Hillsborough and Heysel tragedies and both infrastructure and the understanding of how crowds behave have been enhanced. As the 2022 Champions League final in Paris showed though, there is always room for improvement and authorities often have the instinct to leap to quick and easy conclusions to save face.

Season	Player	Goals
2002/03	Michael Owen	19
2003/04	Michael Owen	16
2004/05	Milan Baroš	9
2005/06	Steven Gerrard	10
2006/07	Dirk Kuyt	12
2007/08	Fernando Torres	24
2008/09	Steven Gerrard	16
2009/10	Fernando Torres	18
2010/11	Dirk Kuyt	13
2011/12	Luis Suárez	11
2012/13	Luis Suárez	23
2013/14	Luis Suárez	31
2014/15	Steven Gerrard	9
2015/16	Roberto Firmino	10
2016/17	Philippe Coutinho/Sadio Mané	13
2017/18	Mohamed Salah	32
2018/19	Sadio Mané/Mohamed Salah	22
2019/20	Mohamed Salah	19
2020/21	Mohamed Salah	22
2021/22	Mohamed Salah	23
2022/23	Mohamad Salah	19

Goals   0   5   10

LIVERPOOL'S LEADING GOAL SCORERS BY ★ SEASON ★

(PREMIER LEAGUE)

★ IAN RUSH ★

The phenomenal goal-scoring capacity of Ian Rush is an intrinsic part of the Liverpool story. Joining the club in 1980 from Chester City, it's hard to believe it took the teenager nine appearances to register his first goal. Once he'd honed his instincts on the big stage, though, he quickly developed a fearsome reputation as one of Liverpool's finest, forming a strike partnership with Kenny Dalglish that is still venerated today. He was the first British player to win Europe's Golden Boot.

Back in the days when you could get a mug of tea and a hot pie on the stands and still see change from a quid, Rush's £300,000 move from Chester City made him the most expensive teenager in the world. Despite this, manager Bob Paisley didn't pick him for the first three months of his contract. When he still wasn't in the first team at the start of the next season, a fuming Rush started to push for a transfer. Paisley, who never had any intention of letting Rush move on, agreed to have discussions, but by the end of the season, Rush had been revved up enough to score 30 goals in 49 appearances and firmly established himself in Liverpool's first team.

In 1983/84, he helped Liverpool win the league for the third consecutive time, retain the League Cup and win the European Cup. In the process, he also knocked in four against Everton as part of a 5–0 demolition of the Toffees, which helped bring his total for the season to 47 goals in 65 games.

Rush played a key role in the legendary Liverpool team of the 1980s, becoming the team's second highest all-time league scorer. In total, he helped Liverpool lift 20 trophies during his time at the club, namely: the Football League First Division five times in 1981/82, 1982/83, 1983/84, 1985/86 and 1989/90; the FA Cup three times in 1985/86, 1988/89 and 1991/92; the League Cup five times in 1980/81, 1981/82, 1982/83, 1983/84 and 1994/95; the Football League Super Cup in 1985/86; the FA Charity Shield four times in 1982, 1986 (shared), 1989 and 1990 (shared); and the European Cup twice in 1980/81 and 1983/84.

He also encouraged a generation to drink more milk.

Football history could have been very different if the mooted move to Crystal Palace had gone through, so the next time a new striker arrives and doesn't instantly set the Kop alight, think back to Ian Rush, the legend who didn't score on his first nine appearances.

"AS WE WENT OUT ON THE PITCH HE HANDED ME A PIECE OF PAPER. IT WAS THE EVENING MENU FOR THE LIVERPOOL ROYAL INFIRMARY."

Jimmy Greaves reminiscing about a tough Anfield welcome from Tommy Smith.

Player	Club
Michael Owen	Liverpool, Newcastle United, Manchester United, Stoke City
Jermain Defoe	Bournemouth, Sunderland, Tottenham Hotspur, Portsmouth, West Ham, Charlton Athletic
Robbie Fowler	Liverpool, Leeds, Manchester City, Blackburn Rovers
Thierry Henry	Arsenal
Frank Lampard	West Ham, Chelsea, Manchester City
Sergio Agüero	Manchester City
Andrew Cole	Sunderland, Portsmouth, Manchester City, Fulham, Blackburn Rovers, Manchester United, Newcastle United
Wayne Rooney	Everton, Manchester United
Harry Kane	Tottenham Hotspur
Alan Shearer	Blackburn Rovers, Newcastle United

Goals

PREMIER LEAGUE'S
★ TOP SCORERS ★

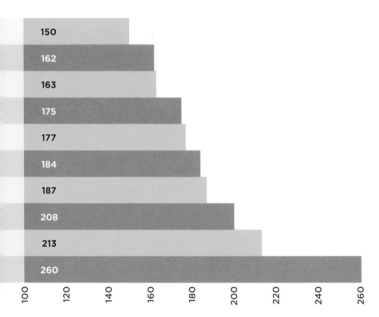

150
162
163
175
177
184
187
208
213
260

100 120 140 160 180 200 220 240 260

★ LIVERPOOL FC WOMEN ★

The women's game has become an increasingly important part of football over the last few years, particularly with the Lionesses overcoming Germany and being crowned champions of Europe in 2022. More than 17 million people tuned in to watch the final and 150,000 girls are now estimated to be playing the sport regularly.

Liverpool's female team has been around since 1989 and became formally associated with the club five years later. They spent the 1990s playing at the top level of women's football, coming second in the FA Women's Premier League in the 1994/95 season (although they were 13 points off the pace).

The 2000s saw the team divide their time between the First and Second Divisions, but they came up as champions three times and reached the semi-finals for the FA Cup twice. They settled into the top flight in the 2010s, winning the championship in consecutive years in 2012/13 and 2013/14 (ending Arsenal's dominance of the competition in the process), although they dropped down to the Second Division at the end of the 2019/20 season. They are currently back in the Women's Super League.

Part of the reason for the sport's massive growth over the last few years is that the Football Association (FA) in England has actually got behind it and made it a formal part of its activities. Women's football had been popular across the UK from the 1880s and enjoyed a surge in popularity during World War I, but in 1921 the FA removed its support on the grounds that, basically, football really wasn't the sort of thing that young ladies should be indulging in.

To be fair, technically they didn't ban women from playing the game; they weren't monsters. They simply banned women from playing football at any association members' grounds – the equivalent of telling women that they were perfectly welcome to water ski anywhere they liked but then taking away access to the water and hiding the skis.

The women's game has sometimes found itself in slightly odd situations within wider society. For example, two years after the FA's ban had been lifted – but still a long way from the women's game being official – England's women faced their Scottish counterparts in 1973. The hotel where they were staying had a policy that stated that girls were not allowed to wear trousers. Why? Because it was a wedding venue and the management didn't want to offend any brides. Things have changed over the last half a century.

The FA's decision to engage with women's football has also led to the righting of some historic wrongs. The women's team of the early 1970s only received their official caps at the back end of 2022. They'd had to provide their own back when they actually played.

LIVERPOOL FC WOMEN'S TEAM IS BASED AT PRENTON PARK, THE HOME OF TRANMERE ROVERS.

"MANY OF THE DREAMS
I HAD WHILE WALKING
THE STREETS OF
BOOTLE AND PLAYING
ON THE PITCHES
HAVE COME TRUE
THROUGH HARD WORK
AND PERSEVERANCE.
CHARACTERISTICS
THAT WERE FORMED IN
BOOTLE."

No matter where she roams,
Alex Greenwood knows where
her home is.

113

★ ALEX GREENWOOD ★

Left and centre back Alex Greenwood has had a varied career. She started out with Everton, joined Notts County, then came to Liverpool where she enjoyed three seasons, scored four goals and delivered several assists.

The Liverpool native has also enjoyed a long career with England, making 73 appearances to date, including being part of the Lionesses' victorious 2019 SheBelieves Cup run and the Euro 2022 campaign. She played in the international side at under-17, under-19 and under-23, before joining the senior squad in 2014. She scored her first England goal in a 10–0 demolition of Montenegro and took the captain's armband at the start of a match for the first time in 2023, having previously worn it after substitutions in other matches.

Since leaving Liverpool, she's enjoyed spells with Manchester United, Olympique Lyonnais and Manchester City, but there's little doubt where her heart lies.

THE OPPOSITION:
★ MANCHESTER CITY ★

Back in the day, Manchester City were a bit like Halley's Comet: they'd turn up in the top league for a little bit, and then, after a couple of seasons, they'd fade and disappear off behind the sun for a while. When they were around, you could always rely on them to stand up to their local rivals, and that usually suited Liverpool just fine.

Their emergence as a force to be reckoned with over the last decade or so has changed the dynamic somewhat.

The two teams first met in the Second Division in 1893, back when City were still calling themselves 'Ardwick'; in total, they've played 223 times in all competitions. Liverpool have won just under half of those meetings.

Looking at the Premier League, it's basically a game of two (slightly uneven) halves. Of the 22 times the two teams met prior to Manchester City's takeover in 2008, Liverpool won around half, drew a little more than a third and did the other thing around 10% of the time. Since 2008, it's become a lot more even, with Liverpool winning around a third of the time, losing a little more than a quarter of the time and honours being shared just under 40% of the time.

While the number of draws has increased, only two of them have been 0-0, so at least there's nearly always a goal to talk about on the way home.

Manchester City is a very different beast from its previous life prior to 2008, but Liverpool still come out on top more of the time. Ultimately, it's a sport – the more competition the better.

★ THE GAP ★

Liverpool spent the best part of three decades at the very pinnacle of English – if not world – football between the 1960s and the 1980s, but it's fair to say that they have faltered slightly in the Premier League era. There have been plenty of trophies, but up to 2019/20, winning the season proved elusive.

If you look at Liverpool's final league positions in each year since the Premier League started in the 1992/93 season, there's an interesting pattern. On average, there has been a 17-point difference between the winner and Liverpool

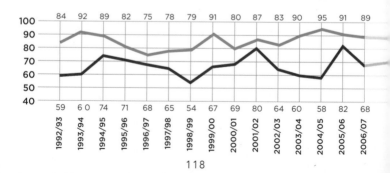

as you can see in the chart below, which shows the final Premier League points total. Over the last decade, that has narrowed to 14 points, but over the last five years, up to the end of the 2022/23 season, the difference has narrowed to eight points.

Three wins between you and the top of the league is basically in contention; just a couple of slip-ups by the leaders and a couple of good days at Anfield and you are there.

Given the amount of money that's sloshing around the Premier League these days, it's unlikely a single team will ever be as dominant for as long as Liverpool were between the 1960s and the 1980s, but if you are mostly only nine points away – three victories – then, let's face it, you are at the races

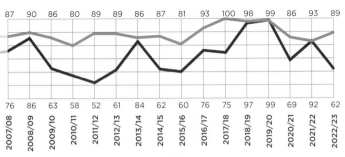

| 87 | 90 | 86 | 80 | 89 | 89 | 86 | 87 | 81 | 93 | 100 | 98 | 99 | 86 | 93 | 89 |

| 76 | 86 | 63 | 58 | 52 | 61 | 84 | 62 | 60 | 76 | 75 | 97 | 99 | 69 | 92 | 62 |

| 2007/08 | 2008/09 | 2009/10 | 2010/11 | 2011/12 | 2012/13 | 2013/14 | 2014/15 | 2015/16 | 2016/17 | 2017/18 | 2018/19 | 2019/20 | 2020/21 | 2021/22 | 2022/23 |

★ JOHN BARNES ★

John Barnes was a bit special when it came to football. He started out on the left wing but moved to central midfield and became a key component of the Liverpool team between 1987 and 1997.

He started his professional career at Vicarage Road, where he spent six years, made 233 appearances and knocked in 65 goals for Watford. During this time, he helped them complete their remarkable five-year rise from the Fourth to the First Division in the late 1970s and early 1980s.

He joined Liverpool for the 1987/88 season, going on to make 314 league appearances, scoring 84 goals and being generally devastating alongside Peter Beardsley during the four years that they were both at Anfield. Barnes went on to become full-time captain of Liverpool after Ian Rush moved on.

Barnes was capped 79 times for England, providing 11 goals and starring regularly in both Euro 88 and the World Cup in 1990. He has also made a rich contribution to the cultural heritage of Great Britain, playing lead roles in both the *Anfield Rap* and *Pass & Move (It's the Liverpool Groove)* as well as New Order's *World in Motion*. He's no Eminem, but having heard Peter Beardsley and Paul

Gascoigne's alternative takes, it's fair to say that Barnes was the pick of the bunch.

Weirdly enough, Barnes' father Ken Barnes, who played for and managed the Jamaican national football team, was also instrumental in the formation of the mid-1980s Jamaican bobsleigh team which was celebrated in the 1993 film *Cool Runnings*.

LIVERPOOL'S FIRST MATCH ONLY HAD 100 FANS IN THE STADIUM, EVEN THOUGH ANFIELD AT THE TIME HAD A CAPACITY OF 20,000. HOWEVER, YEARS LATER, 25,000 PEOPLE CLAIMED TO HAVE BEEN THERE ...

"A WHITE MANAGER LOSES HIS JOB AND GETS ANOTHER JOB, HE LOSES HIS JOB, HE GETS ANOTHER JOB. VERY FEW BLACK MANAGERS CAN LOSE THEIR JOB AND GET ANOTHER JOB."

John Barnes has invaluable perspective.

THE OPPOSITION: ★ CHELSEA ★

Chelsea have a long and distinguished career in the football leagues, but they've not always been able to combine their financial resources and available talent into effective squads. However, there has been plenty of talent wearing both shirts, from Glen Johnson to Joe Cole and Nicolas Anelka (although, to be fair, it sometimes feels like Anelka played for more clubs than Archibald Leitch build stadiums for).

In many ways, the only transfer that really broke the Kop's heart was Fernando Torres' decision to take the Blue, although Mo Salah came the other way a few years later, so it's probably fair to say that Liverpool came out on top there. Objectively. On balance.

The two teams have met 193 times in all competitions since their paths first crossed in 1907, with Liverpool taking the honours around 45% of the time, drawing around a quarter of the time and losing around a third of the time.

Looking at the broad sweep of the Premier League epoch, honours between Liverpool and Chelsea have been fairly evenly split, with Liverpool winning just under 40% of the time and Chelsea winning just under 35% of the time.

Anfield plays a role, with Liverpool winning at home just under half of the time and losing just under half of the time at Stamford Bridge. The 2003 takeover of Chelsea didn't really shift the dial in any particularly meaningful way: Liverpool's proportion of wins has dropped from just over 40% to just over 35%, but what's 5% over the course of 60 and odd games?

There are relatively few 0-0 draws between the pair, but there have only been five matches with more than four goals scored. The average number of goals is slightly less than 2.5 per game, compared to around 2.9 for Arsenal, Spurs and Manchester City, so, basically, stuff happens but there are relatively very few routs.

LIVERPOOL HAVE THE LONGEST UNBEATEN DERBY RUN IN ALL COMPETITIONS, BEATING EVERTON IN 23 CONSECUTIVE GAMES BETWEEN 2011 AND 2020. EVERTON HAD A 16-MATCH UNBEATEN AWAY RUN AGAINST LIVERPOOL BETWEEN 1899 AND 1920.

"TODAY'S TOP PLAYERS ONLY WANT TO PLAY IN LONDON OR FOR MANCHESTER UNITED. THAT'S WHAT HAPPENED WHEN I TRIED TO SIGN ALAN SHEARER AND HE WENT TO BLACKBURN."

Graeme Souness shows why he was never allowed to read the map on the team bus when Liverpool went to away matches.

★ NEIL RUDDOCK ★

Twenty-five years ago, football was a different game. The Premier League was in its infancy, two-footed challenges were part of the fun, and Neil 'Razor' Ruddock was holding the line at Anfield.

Ruddock played for Liverpool between 1993 and 1998, and he embodied the 'work hard, play hard' ethos of the game at the time. Any game that he was involved in could quickly take a turn for the unpredictable, but the moment he became a legend at Anfield in 1994 was during an encounter with Manchester United.

Aware of the risk that Eric Cantona posed to the Liverpool defence, Ruddock decided to rile the flamboyant Frenchman and hopefully make him lose focus on the game. Cantona's famously upturned collar was the symbol of the Manchester United forward's pride, so Ruddock decided to smooth it down for him. At least twice (depending on who is telling the story).

It was an approach that did indeed rile le Cantona, who took a swing at Ruddock. Unfortunately, the Frenchman also scored a last-minute penalty that meant the points were split between the two teams. Ruddock embraced the colourful spirit of the time with gusto, and was, perhaps, an unlikely addition to Liverpool's glamorous Spice Boys – particularly after an off-pitch altercation with Robbie Fowler left Ruddock's expensive boots cut to shreds and Fowler nursing a bloody nose.

In later life, Ruddock has done many things, including recording a charity single with light-entertainment star Peter Andre that may have sold upwards of seven copies, but he'll always be remembered at the Kop as the man who tried to help Cantona look presentable.

JOHN BARNES' RAP IN 'WORLD IN MOTION' WAS WRITTEN BY THE GREAT MAN HIMSELF AND – SO THE STORY GOES – WAS PERFORMED IN ONE TAKE.

"SOMETIMES I WAS RUBBISH, SOMETIMES I WAS ALL RIGHT, BUT IF PEOPLE SEE YOU TRY YOUR HARDEST, NO MATTER WHAT TEAM THEY SUPPORT, THEY LIKE YOU. PLUS, I'M SIX FOOT FOUR AND I LOOK HORRIBLE."

Neil Ruddock was one in a billion. That's probably a good thing.

131

THE OPPOSITION:
★ EVERTON ★

Everton are a team that play in dark blue, have Prince Rupert's Tower – a lock-up – on their badge, used to play at Anfield and mostly play in the English Premier League.

Liverpool have won more than 40% of the nearly 300 matches that the two teams have played down the years, with Everton winning less than 30% of the time. The heaviest defeat Everton have suffered was a match that ended 7–4 in 1933 (discounting matches played during the wars, which were played between sides that were cobbled together by necessity and availability) while Everton's best day against Liverpool came in 1904 when they won 5–2.

In terms of the Premier League, Liverpool win around 45% of the time and honours are shared around 40% of the time.

Despite the hype surrounding the derby, they are generally relatively low-scoring affairs, with around 2.25 goals scored per match and nearly a fifth of matches ending with no score for either side.

Liverpool win at Anfield against Everton more than half the time and win on the other side of Stanley Park a little over a third of the time. There have only been five occasions during the Premier League where more than four goals have been scored.

In the end, Everton is part of Liverpool, and some of Liverpool's most famous players, including Ian Rush, Robbie Fowler and Jamie Carragher, were Evertonian in their youth. There's no reason to hold it against them; they came good in the end.

The Liverpool vs Everton derby is known as the 'friendly derby' because it's basically a chance to wave at your mates across the stadium – and it's probably better that way. Can you imagine what the world would be like if Everton got a sudden influx of money?

LIVERPOOL PLAYED IN WHITE AND BLUE FOR THEIR FIRST FOUR YEARS. EVERTON ALLEGEDLY LEFT THEIR KITS BEHIND WHEN THEY WALKED OUT OF ANFIELD, SO LIVERPOOL PUT THEM TO GOOD USE.

"THERE'S ONLY TWO TEAMS IN LIVERPOOL; LIVERPOOL AND LIVERPOOL RESERVES."

Bill Shankly's world view might have been challenged by the rise of Liverpool FC Women.

· LIVERPOOL ·

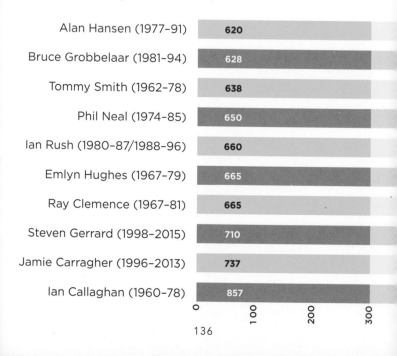

Player	Appearances
Alan Hansen (1977–91)	620
Bruce Grobbelaar (1981–94)	628
Tommy Smith (1962–78)	638
Phil Neal (1974–85)	650
Ian Rush (1980–87/1988–96)	660
Emlyn Hughes (1967–79)	665
Ray Clemence (1967–81)	665
Steven Gerrard (1998–2015)	710
Jamie Carragher (1996–2013)	737
Ian Callaghan (1960–78)	857

LIVERPOOL'S TOP TEN FIRST TEAM ★ APPEARANCES ★

(ALL COMPETITIONS)

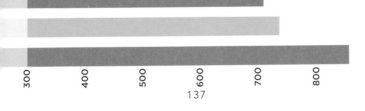

★ROBBIE FOWLER★

138

Robbie Fowler has two reputations. For anyone across the country with a hazy memory of the 1990s, he is remembered as a member of the Spice Boys (see page 75), one of a group of footballers who were thought to be more famous for their exploits on the dance floor than for their achievements on the football pitch. To the red half of Liverpool, however, it's simpler: Robbie Fowler was a phenomenon.

A son of the city, he had two spells at Anfield, from 1993 to 2001 and then from 2006 to 2007, delivering goals of all kinds from all manner of directions. He was clearly a gifted footballer, but he also had an exceptional work ethic, putting in the hours to hone his skills. And it paid off, because no matter what his reputation, he enjoyed a decade-and-a-half's career in the top flight of one of the most demanding football leagues in the world. That's not something you achieve without a decent amount of commitment.

His first spell at Liverpool included 236 league appearances with 120 goals, including a goal on debut and all five in a 5–0 cup win two weeks later. He scored his first league hat-trick on his fifth league appearance, and all in scored 12 goals in his first 13 appearances for the club.

In his first season, he was only one behind Ian Rush as Liverpool's top scorer, cementing his place in the first team for the next seven seasons. He scored more than 30 goals in three consecutive seasons. It might have been a spell with very little silverware, but if you look at any long-term Liverpool goal-scoring stat, there's a decent chance that Fowler's name will be fairly high on the list.

His return to Anfield in 2006 enabled him to score the goals that took him past Kenny Dalglish's all-time top-scoring record, in total scoring 183 goals in 369 appearances. Not bad for a playboy.

"NOTHING HAD CHANGED IN MY ROUTINE, EXCEPT THAT WHEN I WENT DOWN THE CHIPPY AND GOT ME SPECIAL FRIED RICE, IT WOULD BE WRAPPED IN A NEWSPAPER THAT HAD MY PICTURE ALL OVER IT."

Robbie Fowler takes his celebrity status with a pinch of salt and a dash of soy sauce.

PREMIER LEAGUE ERA
★ MANAGERS ★

Liverpool have an excellent record of picking exceptional managers. The exploits of Bill Shankly, Bob Paisley and Kenny Dalglish speak for themselves, but it's also worth noting that, even in the Premier League era, Liverpool have tended to stick with their managers.

Arsenal and Manchester United have had nine permanent managers since 1992. Manchester City have had 16. Spurs have had 46 since last Tuesday. Liverpool have had eight. The Reds haven't been quite as successful as Arsenal, City or United in that time, but the team and the fans have mostly benefited from their loyalty.

On average, Liverpool stick with a manager for three-and-three-quarter seasons before anyone makes an announcement about leaving by mutual consent. The loyalty to managers makes is easier for the players to perform.

Looking back at the broad sweep of Liverpool's history, it's interesting to note that, with the exception of current incumbent Jürgen Klopp – who had an almost preternatural understanding of Anfield from the day that he walked through the door – the best periods of Liverpool's history have been when the team is in the hands of either someone local or someone who has played for the club. Given that some members of the current crop of players are reaching the ends of their careers, and a few have only recently retired, there's plenty of reason to hope that Liverpool will be led by someone with strong links to the club once again ... although let's get at least a few more trophies out of Klopp first.

Season	Month hired	Manager
1992/93	Aug-92	Graeme Souness
1993/94	Feb-94	Roy Evans
1998/99	Aug-98	Roy Evans/Gérard Houllier
1998/99	Dec-98	Gérard Houllier
2003/04	Jun-04	Rafael Benítez
2009/10	Jul-10	Roy Hodgson
2010/11	Feb-11	Kenny Dalglish
2011/12	Jun-12	Brendan Rodgers
2015/16	Oct-15	Jürgen Klopp

THE OPPOSITION: ★ MANCHESTER UNITED ★

When the provisional Premier League fixtures are announced in June, there are two fixtures that most people will have at least a glance at: Liverpool vs Manchester United and Manchester United vs Liverpool. Everton fans, Manchester City stalwarts and proud Gunners all sneak a glance in the direction of the north-west derby.

Why? Because any time that Liverpool and Manchester United meet, sparks are probably going to fly. Sometimes that leads to sublime football, sometimes an unseemly brawl, and usually it leads to Graeme Souness and Roy Keane glowering at each other like two territorial cats in a football analysis studio somewhere, but no matter what happens, there is always going to be something to watch.

(However, there are rumours – started right at this moment, right on this page – that Souness and Keane aren't technically safe to be in the same room during a north-west derby, so they are secretly filmed separately against a blue screen and their discussions edited together through the magic of television. It's why they never quite look each other in the eye, and why you often see the same seagull fly left to right in the background two minutes and 23 seconds into their analysis. Chow on that QAnon.)

Looking at the numbers, honours have been fairly evenly split since the pair first met in 1894, with Liverpool winning around a third of the time, drawing just under 30% and doing the thing that they really didn't do on Sunday 5 March 2023 a bit over a third of the time.

In terms of the Premier League, Manchester United's dominance during the 1990s and 2000s makes the numbers less than pleasant reading from a Liverpool point of view, so let's do the sensible thing and focus on the last decade, where Liverpool have come out on top around 40% of the time and drawn 30% of the time. You can do the maths for the last bit.

In a lot of ways, though, people don't come to a Liverpool vs Manchester United match and expect stats, logic and predictable scorelines. They come for the passion and the incident. Which in some ways is just as well, because the game throws up a fairly average number of 0-0s, the average number of goals is only slightly above 2.5 per game and you've only got a 30% chance of seeing more than three goals.

But people don't come for that sort of thing; they come to see how one team can get in the way of the other. To find out which team is ready for the contest and which is overhyped. To see who is going to hold it together in the first half and then suffer a humiliating rout in the second half ...

"A MATE OWNED A [MANCHESTER UNITED CAPTAIN] BRYAN ROBSON TOP. WE WERE KICKING ABOUT, AND I ASKED IF I COULD BE ROBBO FOR A WHILE. MY DAD LOOKED OUT AND WENT BALLISTIC. HE WASN'T HAVING HIS KID DRAGGING THE GERRARD NAME THROUGH THE GUTTER. I THOUGHT WE'D HAVE TO MOVE!"

Steven Gerrard explains a secret family shame.

147

★ STEVEN GERRARD ★

In a team of phenomenal footballing talents, Steven Gerrard more than holds his own. He made 504 league appearances for Liverpool over a 17-year period with the club, finding the net 120 times. He won the FA Cup twice, the Football League Cup three times, the FA Community Shield, the UEFA Cup and the UEFA Super Cup.

He was 'Man of the Match' in the European Champions League final in 2005, when Liverpool found themselves three goals behind AC Milan after the first half. Led by Gerrard, Liverpool drew level in an astonishing five-minute spell in the second half before winning on penalties. There were several incredible performances on that night in Istanbul. Gerrard's was undoubtedly the best of them.

He was also a mainstay of the England team between 2000 and 2014, making 114 appearances, putting in 21 goals and setting up many more.

With his playing days behind him, he has made the move into management with varying degrees of success. He led Rangers to an undefeated Scottish Premiership title in 2020/21 and clearly has an exceptional footballing brain, so there is little doubt that he will embrace his next challenge when it emerges.

MANCHESTER UNITED AND LIVERPOOL – AN ★ HISTORIC RIVALRY ★

The rivalry between Liverpool and Manchester goes a bit deeper than the exploits of two of the world's most successful football teams. Back in the 19th century, the two cities played important roles in Britain's Industrial Revolution: Liverpool's massive port fed raw materials to Manchester's thriving textile factories and shipped their finished items off around the world. To support this relationship, the Bridgewater Canal, the Mersey and Irwell Navigation and the world's first inter-city railway were built. In 1894, though, the Manchester Ship Canal was completed and a whole lot of business that had been going through Liverpool suddenly shifted 30 miles to the north-east.

This was just as Liverpool FC was getting off the ground, so right from the get-go there was needling between the two groups of fans. Now, obviously, this was long ago and generations away, but it laid the foundations for a rivalry that was then built up by both teams' successes over the latter half of the 20th century. The two teams have won 139 major footballing titles (and that's excluding Second Division titles), and there's a fairly decent chance that they have been competing against each other at some point for the majority of that silverware.

The 1960s gives a good example of this, with the First Division trophy swapping between the two teams each year between 1963/64 and 1966/67 as Liverpool began to establish themselves as the dominant football team of the 1970s and 1980s. It's worth mentioning that despite all the rivalry and the dominance of Liverpool and Manchester United over the years, the two teams have only finished first and second once in the Premier League, in 2008/09.

The history of the fixture is littered with incidents. Who could forget Nemanja Vidić receiving red cards in three consecutive matches between the two teams in 2008/09 and 2009/10? Or the moment that Paul Scholes reacted to Xabi Alonso's perfectly innocent tug on his shirt with what would have been a decent right hook if he'd actually connected? Or the time that Neil Ruddock tried to encourage Eric Cantona to smarten up a bit (see page 127)? Or those seven moments of magic that happened on Sunday 5 March 2023?

The list of things that have happened during Liverpool's matches with Manchester United is long and sometimes entertaining. There has also sometimes been an unpleasant undertone, not just on the pitch but also in the stands – with unpleasant chants about tragic incidents that both clubs have in their histories. It's better when both sides keep the rivalry entertaining.

All that said, matches between Liverpool and Manchester United are likely to continue to be high points in terms of entertainment and represent pivotal moments in all competitions well into the future.

"FEAR IS NOT SOMETHING WE FEEL AT LIVERPOOL."

Is Virgil van Dijk suggesting that all Liverpool players have their amygdalae surgically removed?

★ VIRGIL VAN DIJK ★

Virgil van Dijk joined Liverpool in the January transfer window in the 2017/18 season. He is the first player to have scored against Everton in their debut match since Bill White in 1901.

He subsidised his early career washing dishes in a restaurant in his hometown in the Netherlands. Apparently, his boss tried to discourage him from chasing his football ambitions, telling him he'd be better off staying in the kitchen and earning a few euros.

Ignoring this, van Dijk moved through the ranks at Groningen, Celtic and Southampton, building a reputation that eventually caught the eye of Liverpool. He has now made over 150 league appearances for the Reds, bringing confidence and composure to the heart of the defence.

So far, he has been involved with teams that have delivered a long-dreamed-of Premier League title in 2019/20, an FA Cup and EFL Cup double in 2021/22, an FA Community Shield in 2022, the UEFA Champions League in 2018/19, a UEFA Super Cup in 2019 and a FIFA Club World Cup in 2019. He's also received 54 caps for the Netherlands national team.

Player	Club
Bryan Robson	West Bromwich Albion, Manchester United, Middlesborough
Billy Wright	Wolverhampton Wanderers
Frank Lampard	West Ham, Chelsea, Manchester City
Bobby Charlton	Manchester United
Ashley Cole	Arsenal, Chelsea, Derby County
Bobby Moore	West Ham, Fulham
Steven Gerrard	Liverpool
David Beckham	Manchester United
Wayne Rooney	Everton, Manchester United, Derby County
Peter Shilton	Leicester City, Stoke City, Nottingham Forest, Southampton, Derby County, Plymouth Argyle, Wimbledon, Bolton Wanderers, Coventry City, West Ham United, Leyton Orient

Caps

ENGLAND
CAPS
★ CHART ★

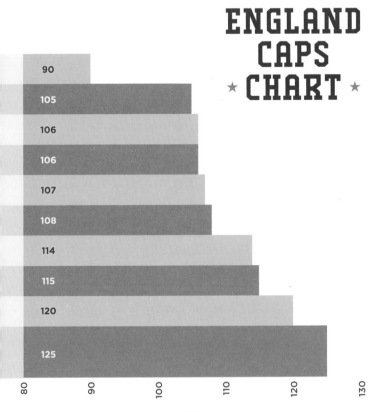

90	
105	
106	
106	
107	
108	
114	
115	
120	
125	

80 · 90 · 100 · 110 · 120 · 130

★ MOHAMED SALAH ★

It could be suggested that Chelsea sometimes have more money than sense. There's a long list of exceptional footballers who had unsuccessful stints in west London. You might have heard of Manchester City's Kevin De Bruyne, but you'll certainly have heard of Liverpool's Mohamed Salah.

Salah started his career at Al Mokawloon, joined Basel after two years and then joined Chelsea a couple of years after that. Struggling for game time, he went out on loan to Fiorentina and Roma, eventually joining the latter permanently.

In 2017, he joined Liverpool – and he hasn't looked back, earning more Premier League Golden Boots than he has feet.

Salah is unsurprisingly a stalwart of the Egyptian team, playing 89 games and scoring 51 times.

It would be easy to turn this into a long list of the accolades he has won and records that he has broken, but let's leave it with this ... During his time at Anfield, Mo Salah has received more bookings for removing his shirt after scoring against Manchester United (2) than Manchester United have scored goals against Liverpool at Anfield while he's been on the pitch (1).

THE TROPHY CABINET ★

Competition	Year
First Division/ Premier League	1900/01, 1905/06, 1921/22, 1922/23, 1946/47, 1963/64, 1965/66, 1972/73, 1975/76, 1976/77, 1978/79, 1979/80, 1981/82, 1982/83, 1983/84, 1985/86, 1987/88, 1989/90, 2019/20
Second Division	1893/94, 1895/96, 1904/05, 1961/62
FA Cup	1964/65, 1973/74, 1985/86, 1988/89, 1991/92, 2000/01, 2005/06, 2021/22
Football League Cup/EFL Cup	1980/81, 1981/82, 1982/83, 1983/84, 1994/95, 2000/01, 2002/03, 2011/12, 2021/22
FA Charity Shield/FA Community Shield	1964*, 1965*, 1966, 1974, 1976, 1977*, 1979, 1980, 1982, 1986*, 1988, 1989, 1990*, 2001, 2006, 2022 (*shared)
European Cup/UEFA Champions League	1976/77, 1977/78, 1980/81, 1983/84, 2004/05, 2018/19
UEFA Cup/UEFA Europa League	1972/73, 1975/76, 2000/01
UEFA Super Cup	1977, 2001, 2005, 2019
FIFA Club World Cup	2019